JOY to YOU and ME

Three Worship Dramas for Christmas

Gurden Henley

C.S.S. Publishing Co., Inc.

Lima, Ohio

JOY TO YOU AND ME

S86 2T

6846 / ISBN 978-0-89536-832-4   PRINTED IN U.S.A

Table of Contents

Author's Introduction

It was twenty-five years ago, when I was a fledgling pastor, that I was first introduced to the effectiveness of drama in the Christian worship service. A young lady who was new to our congregation had been very active in high school and college drama, and wanted to do something for Christmas that year in the way of a play. Not a musical . . . not a pageant . . . but a drama. She gave me a simple play script to read. I was not overly impressed with the play, but thought it sounded a bit interesting, and even consented to be one of the members of the cast. The play went off without a hitch, and I made a great discovery . . . the people talked about the play for weeks after. They examined the experiences in the play, likened them to their own lives, and shared such things as, "you know, how the character in the play reacted is how we, as Christians, should react." I found them talking about and learning from this drama for weeks, when they could hardly remember, from Sunday to Sunday, my best work in sermonizing.

When I saw the effectiveness of drama, I began searching for other plays . . . good plays with "heart" that really made you think, made you cry, made you laugh.

I made the sad discovery that most religious plays were tamed down so that the "laugh lines" would only give the audience a sweet smile . . . one that would be fully acceptable on the "holy ground" of a church platform. I also discovered that most religious plays were written extremely carefully not to arouse too much emotion. We wanted tears in our eyes when we went to a theatre or movie, but not at church. Becoming disgusted with the watered-down versions of religious drama, I began writing my own plays and directing them. Folks in the area soon learned that when we performed a play, it would be fun, interesting, and would have "heart." The crowds came. We had repeat performances, toured with the plays, performed them on television, and turned away hundreds of people from our church that seats 1100, on the nights when the plays were presented.

Then, the "mini-play" was born in my heart. These are plays that I use as an appendix to a holiday sermon . . . and these are what this book is all about.

When Joseph Doubted

Cast (in order of appearance)

MARY
JOSEPH
INNKEEPER
SHEPHERDS

Production Notes

This drama contains a message for every person who has ever entertained a doubt about the Nativity or, in fact, about any other area of religious experience. And, which of us has not had our times of doubts?

When we first performed this little play, I had a slight fear that some in the audience would not appreciate the possibility of Joseph and Mary being less than perfect, and entertaining a doubt or two.

We have now performed it several times before large audiences, and the response has always been very positive. People make such comments as, "Now I can see that belief may not have come so easy for them, either."

Once again, we use live animals in this production. Just a word about that . . . I cannot recommend it highly enough. There simply is no better way to "put your congregation in a stable."

Here is how we go about using live animals: We are fortunate to be located so close to Hollywood. Just a few miles from our church is the Hollywood Wild Animal Training Center, from which we rent most of our animals. But, we have also borrowed some from our church members. (Of course, not just everyone has a camel . . . but, donkeys, sheep or chickens are easier to come by.) We also hire the animal trainer. We have learned that the animals behave better if someone with whom they are familiar stays with them. We place a biblical robe on the trainer, and allow him or her to sit on the floor beside the animal while it is onstage. This does not detract from the production, and we have a much quieter animal.

It also makes for a great deal of excitement to see a camel or two or donkeys and sheep, with trainers in Bible costumes, sitting on the front lawn of the church. We have actually had people who do not attend our church go home, change clothes, and come back for our second or third service on those occasions.

We prepare the stage for animals by placing two thicknesses of green canvas over our green carpet, and then a bit of straw is strewn on the canvas. We also usually build a bit of a fence around the animal . . . it gives nice effect of a stable, and also keeps the animal a bit calmer.

We lead the animal onto the stage just before the beginning of the presentation, and remove him as quickly as possible afterward. We have never had an animal up-stage us by defecating during the performance. Of course, we are prepared for that possibility, and I am sure the audience would take it in stride. After all, that is the stigma of Jesus' being born in a stable.

I have watched the animals in Dr. Robert Schuller's Crystal Cathedral's "Glory of Christmas." Often these animals defecate on stage, and no one seems to mind at all . . . it only adds a bit more realism.

Animals can be rented in most metropolitan areas from petting zoos. They usually have lambs and a donkey. These animals are used to being around people, and perform well. In a rural area, a sheep or donkey can often be borrowed from some of the local folk, who would feel very proud to have an animal in your production, and might even invite all their friends and relatives to come to your Christmas production to see their sheep!

Setting: *A stable with straw and at least one manger. (If possible, consider using a live donkey or sheep or two.)*

Mary

(Laying baby on manger) He's asleep, Joseph! Baby Jesus is asleep, just like any normal baby . . . and he has five toes on each little foot, and five fingers on each hand, and little finger nails, and . . . well, he seems to be a normal child in every way. I had so wondered how the Son of God would look. *(Notices that Joseph is preoccupied)* Joseph, you aren't even listening!

Joseph

Oh . . . yes, yes I am.

Mary

You've been strangely quiet all evening. Aren't you excited?

Joseph

(Not convincingly) Oh yes, yes of course.

Mary

You certainly could have fooled me! Joseph, it is not like you to be so . . . so moody. What's the matter?

Joseph

(Trying to change the subject) Now that the baby is asleep, don't you think we should try to get a little sleep also? It has been a grueling day and night. You must be extremely tired!

Mary

Joseph, you're evading the issue. *(Tenderly)* What's the

matter, sweetheart? And, don't tell me everything's all right, for I know better. You act as though you are disappointed that the awaited child is here.

Joseph
No, that's not it at all.

Mary
Then tell me . . . what is bothering you?

Joseph
Well, to be honest, I am disappointed!

Mary
Disappointed? But he is a perfect child!

Joseph
Not disappointed with the baby! I am disappointed with the Lord!

Mary
Joseph, you can't be serious!

Joseph
Remember, Mary, I'm not the one who wanted to talk about it. But you insisted that I bare my heart. (He turns away from her) Yes, I am disappointed with the Almighty.

Mary
How can you say that after what has happened here this evening?

Joseph
It's because of what happened here, that I say this! Why

would the God of the Universe, with all of his wealth, might, power, and riches, allow his Son to be born in a smelly place like this? *(Questioningly)* If it is his Son!

Mary

(In great astonishment) Joseph! How can you say such a thing?

Joseph

You deserve better than this, Mary! *(Pointing to child)* He deserves better than swaddling clothes, even if he isn't the Son of God!

Mary

(In greater astonishment) Joseph!

Joseph

(Continues, without even pausing) I tried to do better for you! Even a poor carpenter tried to get a room in the inn for a birthplace. *(A bit angry)* No decent father would allow this to happen if he had the power to help it. The only people who frequent this place, other than those smelly stable boys, are the maids at the inn who, for a few sheckles bring the half-drunken caravaneers here as a trysting place for lust. This certainly is not the kind of place I would pick for the birth of my son. Can you still believe that the child is the Son of God?

Mary

Joseph — you can't know what you are saying! If this is not the Son of God, then you are saying that I am immoral . . . and that this child has no known father.

Joseph
When you put it that way, it sounds rather harsh. But that, in truth, is what I am thinking.

Mary
Joseph, can't you see. . . the birth of this *boy* baby is just another confirmation.

Joseph
Yes, I thought of that. If it had been a girl, it would have . . .

Mary
(Interrupting him) Joseph, how can you doubt? Have you forgotten that an angel came to you and told you to marry me . . . told you that the baby is the Son of God? *(Looks away from him)* I have never doubted. I have kept all of these things in my heart, and pondered them. My faith grew with every movement of the child within me. *(Pleading)* Joseph, I am not an immoral woman! Joseph, this child is the Son of God!

Joseph
I, too, once believed that with all my heart. But now . . . I must confess that I have some doubts about whether an angel actually came to me or not. It was a dream, you know . . . and perhaps I read more into it than I should have, because I was so bewildered by your condition . . . because I loved you so much . . . because I did not want to hurt you. Mary, I wanted to believe you. For a long time, I was convinced that it was more than a dream — it was an angel sent from God. But now I have so many doubts. If it was from God, I feel that he has failed me.

Mary

(Surprised) Joseph!

Joseph

For seven months, silence! The entire time we were bearing the jeers of our friends, even our families' suspicions . . . not a word from God. And then, being called on to come to Bethlehem when you were so near the time of birth. It just wasn't right for you to have to make this trip! I was positive God would prevent your having to come. Did he want his Son born in this hamlet? I can hardly believe that. And, while we were making the trip . . . all of those elegantly saddled caravans we passed, and us trudging along in the dust and heat with only a donkey! I kept thinking that one of them might ask us to ride with them . . . I even half expected that we would miraculously come upon two white camels, saddled with velvet, prepared by God for us to make the trip. But, nothing! God did nothing special . . . even after the angel told us that we were highly favored people! (A bit sarcastic) Highly favored, all right!

Mary

Joseph, you, too, are tired. It is easy for doubts to rise when the body is weary. You will feel better in the morning.

Joseph

For days I have believed in — and prayed for — some miracle to give me assurance. I really wanted to believe my experience, Mary. All I needed was a sign from God. Even a small sign would have been sufficient. When the innkeeper said there was no room in the inn, I persuaded him to go and check just one more time to make sure . . . I was convinced that God was going to perform a miracle, and give us one of the better rooms for his Son to be born in. *(Sarcastic)* Would that have been too hard for the Almighty? But, nothing! And then, when in desperation I had to bring you here to this dreadful place, it was with greatest disappointment. There was nowhere else to go. Then, in the crucial moment when the child was born, my heart pleaded with God to give us a sign. In that moment, just one clap of thunder, or a freak hail storm . . . anything! Just anything! Mary . . . if what we have been led to believe is true, then the birth of this child is the greatest event ever to happen in this world. I cannot imagine the Almighty being silent . . . totally silent! The same silence we have lived with these last months! *(Apologetically)* I am trying to keep faith, Mary. Believe me, I am! But I have questions . . . so many questions!

Mary

It is not a sin for you to have questions, my dear. I have had some, also. I have questioned why the Lord would desire to have his Son born in this stable, in Bethlehem. But, I am certain if we search the Scriptures, we will find it is in fulfillment of prophecy. Remember all of the other Scriptures which have come to life for us during these past nine months? Joseph, you are a good, honest and devout man. God has chosen you to act as the father to his Son. He will not disappoint you, but he'll give you the sign you so desperately need. So, hold fast to your faith, Joseph, hold fast to your faith.

Innkeeper

(Interrupting) Is everything all right out here? *(Looks around)* Seems to be okay. Sorry to bother you, but I saw a strange glow coming into my bedroom window from this direction . . . thought the hay was on fire again. Must have been a glow from that star, and not the hay, after all.

Joseph
A star?

Innkeeper
Just last year we had a terrible fire here, when some drunken caravaneers carelessly caught the hay on fire. It was a disastrous . . .

Joseph
(Interrupting him) A star, you say?

Innkeeper
Oh yes, a mysterious star, kind of hanging-like in the sky. There's also a strange glow over near Boaz's shepherds' fields. Just some freak atmospheric conditions. Well . . . sorry to bother you. Good night. Oh, by the way, come on over to the inn in the morning. I've got some folks checking out, and I may be able to get you a room. Good night, now.

Joseph
(To innkeeper) Good night . . . see you in the morning. (To Mary, excitedly) A mysterious star? Mary, did you hear what he said? Perhaps it is the sign God is giving!

(Shepherds enter)

Shepherd
Excuse us, but we are looking for a baby. Do you know if there is one here?

Joseph
A few hours ago you would have been out of luck. But,

it just so happens that we do have a newborn baby boy.
Jesus is his name.

Shepherd
Is he wrapped in swaddling clothes, and lying in a manger?

Joseph
I'm sorry to say, it is true. We had no choice. We had nothing better to wrap him in, and no other place to lay him.

Shepherd
(As shepherds bow) Then it is true! The Angel told us this would be a sign . . . we would find the baby wrapped in swaddling clothes, and lying in a manger.

Joseph
Angel, you say?

Shepherd
(Choir starts to sing, very softly) Oh, no, not just one . . . the heavens were filled with them. They were singing, "Glory to God in the highest, and on earth, peace . . . for born this day in the City of David, is a Savior, Who is Christ the Lord." (Joseph is ecstatic) Listen . . . you can still hear them singing in the distance (They listen) (Choir softly sings, then gets louder)

Joseph
Those are angels, Mary! Listen! The angels are singing! It is a sign from God. THIS IS THE SON OF GOD! (With tears) Mary, the angels are heralding his birth! JESUS IS THE SON OF GOD!

Off-limits to Shepherds

Cast (in order of appearance)

EZRA
INN KEEPER
LOPSA
JOSEPH
MARY
SHEPHERD I
SHEPHERD II
SHEPHERD III

Production Notes

This play has much audience appeal, and is also fun to produce. We have performed it many times before very large audiences, and have always had excellent responses.

We recommend using a live donkey in this production. There is nothing that can compare to the excitement and atmosphere of the presence of live animals to add to the reality of a nativity drama.

My mini-dramas are always performed at the conclusion of my holiday sermon. On the morning during which we presented this drama, the presentation had just been concluded and we had just, by the magic of our revolving platform, revolved off the set with its animals and costumed characters. There was now just a thin, sterile wall between myself in the pulpit, and the animals. As I began asking the benediction, the donkey began to bray, very loudly and continuously. Of course, I had no choice but to stop my prayer, and laugh with my congregation. The people later agreed that this was the most realistic Christmas service they had ever attended. "It was just like being there when Jesus was born," they said. Certainly, one could expect a donkey in the real stable in which Christ was born to bray at a most inopportune time.

In your casting, it is very important that you find a very out-going actor to play the part of Ezra. The character should be a bit eccentric, and overzealous in his hatred of shepherds. The drama will draw a few good laughs, but will not lose the sensitive, warm touch of the first Nativity, which you desire to portray.

Scene: *The stable where Christ was born. (The stable should be complete with hay or straw and some live animals. A live donkey is a must. The stable should be decorated with a series of signs, "OFF-LIMITS TO SHEPHERDS," "NO SHEPHERDS ALLOWED," "SHEPHERDS KEEP OUT," etc.*

Setting: *The first Christmas.*

Ezra

(Talking to his donkey, which he pats from time to time as he removes a pad-like saddle) I do believe it is finally starting to quiet down a bit. I'll bet you're weary of it all, too, aren't you, Primrose? *(Pats her affectionately)* I know I'll be glad when everybody leaves Bethlehem and goes home. Home . . . now there's a word that brings up memories! Well, they should be glad they have a home to go to! The Romans did more than place a new tax on me . . . they destroyed everything I ever had! *(begins getting louder)* Burned my home . . . massacred my Anna and our children . . . our entire village . . . simply because our village gave food and drink to the band of Zealots that the Romans were chasing. *(Grimaces)* I will never forget the sight that greeted my eyes when I came home from Jerusalem that day! Not just my eyes . . . your eyes, too! You were with me that dreadful day. You'll have to excuse me for shouting at you. I guess you know me well enough to know I don't mean it. It's just that at times it all comes back to me. Nighttime is the worst time. Guess that's because there's more time to think. In the daytime, we're both too busy to think, aren't we, Primrose? Especially at this time, with Caesar's new law bringing people from all over the Middle East to our little Bethlehem. It is strange . . . one wouldn't think that people could get

18

so far removed from their roots . . . but here they come, from everywhere. Why, the inn is absolutely bulging tonight with tired, cranky people! None of them seems happy to have come home. But, then, guess you wouldn't get too excited about having to travel a long way to pay a new tax. That's not the kind of thing that would put people in a good mood, is it, Primrose? The boss must be making a lot of money. Let's see . . . how many times did he send us to the market? More wine . . . more bread . . . more vegetables . . . *(He shouts)* GET MORE FIREWOOD! How many loads of firewood did we carry today, anyway? But, now all is quiet . . . *(Pats donkey again)* That means we should get some sleep. *(He goes over to a mat which is used as a bed, and begins taking off his outer garment.)* Now, Primrose, please don't be stomping all night! I know the stable is full and all of those other animals make you nervous, but we're both in need of our rest. *(Lies down on mat, places outer garment mantle over him.)* It really feels good to be off my feet! *(He is quiet for a moment, then begins to snore.)*

Innkeeper
(Tries to open door, but it is locked; so he knocks loudly and continuously) EZRA! *(Very disgustedly)* Open this door!

Ezra
(Waking abruptly) Yes, I'm coming!

Innkeeper
(Still knocking impatiently) Open this door! Hurry up and unlock this door!

Ezra
(As he opens the door) Yes, boss . . . come on in.

Innkeeper
(*Coming in, with a small, frightened-looking boy by the hand*) How many times have I told you it is not necessary to lock this door? There's nothing in here that anyone would want!

Ezra
But, boss . . . it's those shepherds . . . they might come in while I am asleep. They're such a scummy lot . . . they'll steal anything they can get their hands on!

Innkeeper
Why are you so prejudiced against shepherds? They are just people . . . ordinary people! Some good, some bad . . . just like any other kind of people!

Ezra
Then, why aren't they allowed to give testimony in court? I'll tell you why . . . it's because they're liars . . . they're cheats . . . they're crooks . . . they're foul-mouthed thieves . . . that's what they are!

Innkeeper
True, some are that way . . . but that's no reason to be prejudiced against all of them.

Ezra
I've yet to see a good one!

Innkeeper
(*Purposely changing the subject*) Ezra . . . I found this boy trying to sleep beside the inn. He was all shakey and cold. I thought he might be more comfortable in here with you. Those in the caravan from Mesopotamia which arrived to-

day said he followed them. They couldn't find out who he is, but believe him to be a refugee. They reported seeing many in some of the areas through which they passed . . . people whose families have been destroyed by the Romans or, at best, misplaced. Those in the caravan said that one of the ladies in the group made the mistake of giving this one something to eat, and he just began following them like a stray dog. No matter how hard they tried, they couldn't get rid of him. Some of the men tried throwing rocks at him to make him go home, but they couldn't get rid of him. Obviously, he had no home. When I went out to make my final rounds outside the inn, I saw him huddled up against the building, all shivering . . . I don't know if it is from fear, or from the cold. But, surely, it can't hurt to let him sleep in here by the fire for just one night. *(He starts to leave . . . then calls back)* Oh yes . . . I am sending out another couple also. They have just arrived from Nazareth, and she is expecting a child at any time. The maid is fixing them a bite to eat, and then they will be coming out here. I did not have the heart to send them away . . . not with her expecting a child and all.

Ezra
But where am I supposed to put them?

Innkeeper
(Starts to leave again) You'll manage, Ezra, you'll manage! *(He turns back)* Oh yes . . . I forgot to tell you . . . our young man here, speaks no Hebrew, Arabic nor Greek. The folks with the caravan said they could not figure out which language he does speak. Good night, Ezra!

Ezra
Good night, Sir. *(He closes the door and looks at the boy)* Hello! *(No response)* Hi!

Lopsa

Hi! *(With a big smile)*

Ezra

Hi!

Lopsa

Hi! *(Both smiling)*

Ezra

My name is Ezra. *(No response from the boy)* Mine Numbra est Ezra! *(No response)* Me, Ezra! *(Points to himself)* Ezra . . . Ezra . . . *(Continuing to point to himself)*

Lopsa

(Finally comprehending) E-Z-R-A?

Ezra

(Smiling widely, nodding yes) Yes, Ezra!

Lopsa

Ezra . . . Ezra

Ezra

Yes, and what's your name? *(No response)* You . . . *(Points at Lopsa)* You . . . what's your name?

Lopsa

(Pointing to himself) Sa ben hab? *(Pointing to himself)* Sa ben hab? *(Points to himself again)* Ben Hab . . . Lopsa! *(Points to himself again)* Lopsa!

Ezra

Lopsa?

22

Lopsa

(All smiles) Lopsa, ben hab. *(pointing to himself again)* Lopsa!

Ezra

Well, I don't know about you . . . but I've got a big day tomorrow and I want to get some sleep. *(He goes to his mat, starts to lie down and then notices the boy, just standing there frightened-looking. He gets up, takes the boy to his bed and tucks him in; then goes and sits by the fire with his head in his hands, speaking very softly.)* I think he's asleep, Primrose. Tucking him in like that reminded me of tucking in my own children. Strange . . . every time I think I have those memories buried deep enough that they won't hurt me again, something happens that goes digging them up again. It's those dirty Romans! *(With bitterness)* Oh, how I'd love to place signs all over Palestine, "OFF-LIMITS TO ALL ROMANS". How we need the Messiah to come! *(Breaks forth into a brief Prayer)* Oh, Lord, send the promised Deliverer! How long? How long must we wait? *(Pauses for a brief moment)* Well, Primrose, we must get some sleep . . . got a big day tomorrow. *(Goes to sleep and once again begins to snore. Soft knock on the door by Joseph and Mary, who are waiting outside, wakes him. He is startled and unhappy with the interruption)* I'm coming . . . I'm coming! Maybe the boss is right . . . should just leave this door unlocked. *(As he opens door)* You must be the couple the boss told me about. Come on in.

Joseph

I am Joseph, and my wife's name is Mary. The innkeeper told us we might stay here tonight.

Ezra

Yes. . . *(Yawning)* Yes. . . he told me you were coming.

Joseph

It is so kind of you to allow us to spend the night. Some private corner of the stable is all we'll require.

Ezra

Yes, yes . . . *(Yawning again)* Here's a lamp. You can have the entire backside of the stable to yourselves . . . *(Laughs)* That is, if you don't count camels and donkeys. *(Joseph and Mary exit to back, Joseph holding up the lantern and carrying a large bundle, plus helping Mary along.)* Good night. I'll keep the fire going all night. If you should get chilly, you can come out here and warm yourselves.

Joseph

Thank you, sir. Good night!

Ezra

(Settling in again by the fire, speaking softly to the donkey) Primrose, are you asleep yet? You're lucky . . . you can sleep standing up. What are we going to do with the little tyke there on my bed? We can't just send him out into the world with nowhere to go and no one to care. He can't just continue chasing after caravans who throw rocks at him trying to get rid of him. Primrose, you know how lonely I have been . . . perhaps I should . . . Oh, yes, I know I've got you, but sometimes you just sleep while I'm talking to you. I always did envy your ability to sleep while you are standing up. Yes, Primrose . . . he does need somebody! *(Giving a big yawn)* Lucky you. . . . sleeping while you are standing . . . *(He begins to snore. Then, a baby's cry can be heard. He is awakened,*

shows a bit of disgust) Who can possibly sleep around here?
(Begins to stoke the fire)

Joseph

Oh, I'm so glad to see that your're awake. I was afraid the
baby's fussing might wake you up. Would you mind if we
came nearer to the fire? It is very chilly back there.

Ezra

Of course, I wouldn't mind! *(Joseph goes and helps Mary
come to center stage and the fire. Mary is holding a baby)*
I'll build the fire up a little bigger. Well . . . is it a boy or
girl? *(Little boy props himself up on his elbows and watches)*

Joseph

He's a fine boy! Just like the angel said! *(Mary smiles)* We
named him Jesus. Rather . . . God named him Jesus!

Ezra

Jesus means "Savior." But, what do you mean, "God
named him"?

Joseph

It may be hard for you to believe this, him being born under these conditions and all, but you are looking into the
face of the Messiah!

Ezra

I suppose every Jewish father and mother hope that. I
know I did. But, look . . . my children were destroyed before they even came to years.

Joseph

But it's true! Time will tell.

Ezra

You need a place to lay him. I made a portable manger for Primrose. Do you suppose it might work for a cradle? *(He brings it and fluffs up the straw)* Not much, but guess it will do.

Mary

It's very nice, thank you! *(Lopsa brings outer garment he has been wrapped up in, and lays it on the straw)* Thank you, son . . . that is very sweet of you.

Ezra

No use talking to him. He doesn't understand any of the languages we know. He doesn't understand anything.

Mary

Everyone understands this in any language . . . *(She hugs him. He beams, and leans into her, obviously enjoying it)*

Ezra

Say, I've got something that I think was saved for this very night. *(He goes and gets an ornate box, and pulls from it some white cloth and a little boy's garment)* Swaddling cloth, left over from when I buried my family. Perhaps it would do to wrap the baby in. He needs something soft next to his little body. And, here, Lopsa, the one garment I saved from my son. It might be a bit big, but I think you can wear it. *(Mary takes the swaddling cloth and wraps the baby in it, then lays him in the manger. Lopsa is elated with the robe, and puts it on. There is a knock at the door)* Come in! *(Three shepherds begin to come in, one carrying a lamb. Ezra sees that they are shepherds, and is immediately on his feet, pushing them out the door.)* Uh . . . no . . . don't come in! No shepherds are allowed here!

Joseph

(*Trying to intervene*) But, why can't they come in?

Ezra

Can't you see the sign? This place is off-limits to shepherds. (*Lopsa is at the door and takes it that he is being shouted at to leave, so he exits.*) Get out! Beat it! (*The shepherds refuse to go, and speak to Joseph around Ezra who is still shouting at them to go.*)

Shepherd I

But, we only need to ask a question and, if the answer is "no", then we will gladly be on our way.

Ezra

(*Standing in front of them, preventing them from moving ahead*) What is your question? Ask it, then be on your way.

Shepherd II

Is there a new-born baby boy here, and is he wrapped in swaddling clothes?

Ezra

Why yes, there is. Uh, but how did you know?

Shepherd I

An angel told us. Not just one angel . . . (*They all press forward toward the baby, passing by Ezra who is in a state of shock.*)

Shepherd III

The sky was full of angels!

Shepherd I

They were all singing, and saying, "Glory to God in the highest, and on earth, Peace, good will to men."

Shepherd II

They told us to go to Bethlehem, and this would be a sign to us . . . we would find the babe wrapped in swaddling clothes, and lying in a manger. We stopped at several stables, but no baby. Then we saw the star over this one and, sure enough, just as the angel said!

Shepherd I

The angel told us . . . "FOR UNTO YOU IS BORN THIS DAY, IN THE CITY OF DAVID, A SAVIOR WHO IS CHRIST THE LORD!" He was talking to us shepherds. Then he said that the news was to ALL PEOPLE! He included us shepherds. I don't know why he came to us, unless it was to let the world know he had come to everyone be they a king or even a shepherd.

Ezra

Now you've told your story, so get out!

Shepherd III

(Ignoring Ezra) I brought my best lamb as an offering to the Messiah. (He gives the lamb to Joseph, then kneels in front of the manger)

Ezra

(Becoming very upset) How did this ever happen? Shepherds in my stable! Oh, no . . . they'll walk off with everything that's not tied down! (Begins putting things away, starting with his ornate box) How disgusting! Shepherds in my stable!

Shepherd I

We worship our Messiah. The angel said, "A Savior, Who is Christ the Lord." (Door flies open, and Lopsa runs in, gesturing excitedly)

Lopsa

Peen ta la Fraken! Peen Ta La Fraken. *(Gesturing with hands, making a star high in the air, and then showing its rays coming down)* Peen Ta La Fraken! *(He takes Ezra by the hand and leads him outside. In a moment they both come back in, very excited.)*

Ezra

A star! Not just a star . . . a mysterious star!

Lopsa

La Fraken!

Ezra

An amazing star! The most brilliant star you've ever seen, almost like the sun! With shooting rays coming down and lighting up my stable. It's amazing!

Shepherd I

We told you! The star guided us here . . . otherwise we would still be checking out stables for a baby wrapped in swaddling clothes.

Shepherd II

See, the Messiah has come! *(Shepherds kneel in worship. Before Ezra kneels, he goes and pulls down all of the signs forbidding shepherds to enter; then he goes and kneels beside the shepherds. He looks up and sees Lopsa standing alone by the door. He motions for him to come to him.)*

Lopsa

(As he goes to Ezra) Peen Ta La Fraken!

Ezra

Peen Ta La Messiah! *(Lopsa kneels beside Ezra, who places an arm around him; then Lopsa puts his arms around Ezra, who has his other arm around a shepherd)*

The Old Torch Lighter

Cast (in order of appearance)

GUARD
SIMEON
JOSEPH
MARY (not a speaking part)

Production Notes

This play requires a Roman-type temple soldier uniform. These can be rented at almost any costume rental agency. Be sure to steer away from the homemade type. I can't begin to tell you how many plays I have seen in which the Roman soldier became a comedy character because his uniform was so tacky and homemade looking. Get an authentic looking uniform . . . one that will nearly take the audiences' breath away if the soldier should face them and bark an order.

We could not find a candle or lamp snuffer of the type we wanted for this drama, even though we are close to Hollywood and have access to all the studio's props and costumes. We made our own snuffer by using an 8-foot piece of dowling, a small tin can, upside down, on the end of the pole beyond the can, and spray painted the entire top of the snuffer with flat black paint to give the appearance of oil smoke.

Setting: Very simple, Roman column, with Roman type bench. *(As the scene opens, Temple Guard Joab walks back and forth in front of pillar a time or two, as if patrolling; then goes and sits on bench, stretches, yawns, takes off his sword, and stretches out on the bench and goes to sleep. Simeon, who is a very old man, comes onto the stage; notices the guard asleep, and touches him with the torch snuffer he has been carrying.)*

Guard

(Quickly and wildly jumping to his feet; looking for his sword and making different hand salutes for each salutation) Hail Caesar . . . eh . . . Long live Herod! . . . Holy Caiaphas . . . *(Noticing who it is)* Oh . . . it is only you, Simeon!

Simeon

You have many allegiances, Joab!

Guard

(Stretching, and once again strapping on his sword) If you are saying I have many bosses, you are right! I must please the Roman Centurion, who is very difficult to please, as he does not think we need a guard for the temple, anyway. I must please my superiors under Herod's command; and then there is old crotchety Annas and his son, Caiaphas, the High Priests, who are most demanding on us that we do not allow any gentiles to enter the temple and defile it.

Simeon

Yes, yes . . .

Guard

Don't get me wrong. I am grateful that I have a job. So many at this time of Roman occupation do not, you know. Simeon . . . do me a favor, and do not report me for . . . *(Motions to seat)* I beg of you!

Simeon

What you do on your shift is between you and your superiors. I am merely about my own morning task . . . and what a beautiful morning it is going to be!

Guard

Yeah . . . and just what's beautiful about it?

Simeon

A new day . . . and with it, a new hope!

Guard

Hope? *(Sarcastically)* Ha! Hopes for what? A new tax decree by the Romans? It seems they have been very clever in devising ways of taxing us. Or perhaps your hope is that Herod will not decide to extend the tragic decree that all boy babies in and around Jerusalem will be destroyed, as he has done at Bethlehem! Hope that . . .

Simeon

(Interrupting) I do believe that Joab did not get his sleep out! *(Laughs softly)* Or, could you have awakened on the wrong side of the bench?

Guard

(Nearly railing on him) You and your hope! *(Extremely sarcastic)* What does your hope hinge upon, old torch lighter? Do you have hope that the Roman Commander

Varsus will not crucify another two thousand of our Zealots again as a warning to our population that Rome will not tolerate our independence?

Simeon

(Grimaces at the thought) You are now getting too close to home, Joab.

Guard

(Not paying attention to the common and obvious hurt of the old man) Did you not lose a relative in that public display of rage? All of the rest of us did! Then we got the news . . . Varsus has decreed that no body can be taken down from the cross. He is determined that they will hang there until they rot down. Now, for days . . . there they hang.

Simeon

(Looking away, but pleading) Please . . .

Guard

(Not even hearing Simeon) Can you go there and look up into those decaying faces . . . and then talk about hope? *(Very sarcastically)* Obviously, you do not have a brother there *(Sarcastic tone turns to hurt)* as I do!

Simeon

(Turning very slowly toward him) No, I do not have a brother . . . I have a son! *(This is spoken in sincerity; not sarcasm)* And you are right, I can no longer bear to go there in the daylight, because I cannot stand to look at the guresome sight. I go at night . . . I have jsut come from the cross of my son, where I knelt and cried out to God to send the promised Deliverer. And now . . . a new day, and a new hope. Perhaps this may just be the day!

Guard

(Apologetically) I am sorry, I did not know . . .

Simeon

I have discovered, Joab . . . the greater the hurt and grief, the greater the need for hope. Your feelings . . . your lack of hope . . . is what is ailing our nation. Far worse the calamity of the loss of faith and hope than the calamity of the Roman occupation with its atrocities. You know Israel has always had problems! Because we are God's Chosen does not mean he has shielded us from all problems. But, we were able to cope, because somewhere we had hope. Always a prophet's voice crying out . . . "AND IT SHALL COME TO PASS . . ." or "AND IN THOSE DAYS . . ." or "BEHOLD THE DAY SHALL COME. . ." — always an eye to the future, with hope. But now, when we need hope more than ever, the religious leaders who once encouraged us are involved in corruption, legality and formality. And our nation's political leaders have lost faith in God; and in their own strength try to weary our oppressors — an action that only leads to the mass crucifixions which have so recently touched all of our lives. Joab . . . keep your faith in God alive, and hope . . . don't lose hope! It is like the torches I light . . . hope brightens the darkest night!

Guard

Is this why you have volunteered to care for the temple torches? I notice you lighting them each evening, and putting them out each morning at daybreak.

Simeon

I am old! I'm not much good for anything! Some small things I can do. The torches had long ago been abandoned

. . . therefore no one came to pray at night. I endeavored
to make it more inviting if someone should choose to come
here to pray at night. You remember, we are to pray for
. . . and hope for . . . the Promised Deliverer. *(Thinks,
then speaks more quietly)* Tonight, as I knelt beneath the
cross upon which hung the body of my son . . . *(Coming
to himself)* . . . Oh, perhaps I should not speak of it . . .

Guard
What were you about to say, Simeon?

(Haltingly) I don't know if I can put it into words . . . or
if I should even try . . . (Pauses)

Guard
Yes, go on. . .

Simeon
(Begins speaking very reverently) It was as I was in prayer
at the foot of the cross of my son . . . I sensed . . . it was
so real . . . It is so difficult to say . . .

Guard
(Encouraging him) Yes. . .?

Simeon
The Almighty was so near, as if he understood my heartache . . . our heartache. As if he knew how it felt to stand
by the cross of a son. And, not only did his presence com-
fort this old man's heart in an indescribable way, but he
also seemed to say, "I not only understand your heartache
in giving up a son, I am also rewarding your faith and hope.
Therefore, you shall not taste of death until your eyes have
beheld your Lord's Christ." *(Excited)* That's what God

spoke to me . . . I would see the Messiah with my own eyes!

Guard

(Disgustedly) Oh, sure . . . Old man, too much sorrow has led you to senility! Too many sleepless nights . . . too many tears . . . (As he is exiting) too much hope!

Simeon

(Calling after him) But, what do we have, if we do not have hope? (His voice trails off into nothingness; he begins to speak to himself) Senile? Could I be getting senile? And, old Anna . . . she is yet older than I . . . could she be senile also? For she yet hopes! She, like I, comes here each day, waiting for the couple who shall bring him who shall be the Messiah! Him who shall be born of a virgin. Him who shall be born in Bethlehem of Ephrata. (He sits on bench, and gets drowsy) Senile, eh? Do you suppose? No! God did speak to me! I will have hope! (He dozes off to sleep)

(Young couple comes onto stage, carrying a baby. Joseph shakes Simeon gently)

Joseph

Excuse us, sir . . . the court where children are presented to the Lord . . . can you tell us how to find it?

Simeon

(Startled, wide-eyed, accommodating) Oh, yes, yes . . . that is what I do best! I have greeted most of the couples who have come to dedicate babies for a couple of years now. (Looking at baby) What a fine young man he is! What is his name?

Joseph

His name is Jesus!

Simeon

(With greater interest) Jesus . . . that means "Savior"! *(More excited)* And, where was your Jesus born, if I may ask?

Joseph

You may not believe it, but he was born in a stable, in Bethlehem.

Simeon

Bethlehem? *(Half to himself)* Could it be? . . . Do you suppose? . . . Could I hold your baby . . . er . . . Jesus?

Joseph

Of course!

Simeon

(Taking the baby into his arms. As he does, a bright light comes on him and the baby. His eyes light up and he speaks to God with great emotion) Lord, let now your servant die in peace, according to your Word. For mine eyes have seen your salvation, which you have prepared before the face of all people. A light to lighten the Gentiles, and the Glory of your people Israel. *(Looking at and speaking to Mary and Joseph)* Forgive the tears of an old man . . . but, once I held my own son high like this, and now he is being held high in another way . . . on one of Varsus' crosses. As I knelt beneath that cross last night, God was there, as if he was experiencing my hurt. Now, as I hold this child . . . I have a strange premonition . . . *(To himself)* No, I must not blight the happy occasion of the dedication of this child. *(To couple)* I will say

this . . . Keep faith! Even though it seems like a sword is piercing your own heart, keep faith! Keep hope. . . that God is come in the form of this child, and that no matter how dark the night may be, God will be in it, bringing salvation. *(Stands awe-struck, not speaking for a moment)*

Joseph
(Takes baby from him) You did say the court for the dedication of infants was this way? *(Simeon comes to his senses and nods. They leave)*

Simeon
(Watching them go, somewhat dazed) Lord God . . . You told me that my eyes would see him, but you have blessed me beyond measure. I have held him in my arms! *(Grabs up candle lighter-snuffer and runs down center aisle)* ANNA . . . My eyes have beheld him! ANNA! HE HAS COME!

www.ingramcontent.com/pod-product-compliance
Lightning Source LLC
Chambersburg PA
CBHW071759020426
42331CB00008B/2327